My Family is PERF

This is my Family.

This is my Dad

and this is my Mum.

My Perfect Family

Written by Timus Radford-Mathurin

Dedicated to,
Tanah, Millie, Amiyah, Myla, Preston & Macey
X

This is my Family.

This is my Mum

and this is my Sister.

My Family is PERFECT!

This is my Family.

This is my Dad

and these are my Brothers.

My Family is PERFECT!

This is my Family.

This is my Mum, this is my Brother

and this is my Step-Dad.

My Family is PERFECT!

This is my Family.

This is my Nan

and this is my Grandad.

My Family is PERFECT!

This is my Family.

These are my two Mums.

My Family is PERFECT!

This is my Family.

These are my Foster Carers.

My Family is PERFECT!

We all have different families,
and that's PERFECTLY ok,

Our families are PERFECT to us
in each and every way...

..and yours is too!

My Perfect Family

Stick your perfect family
photo here and upload it to instagram
#myperfectfamilybook
to join the fun!

Copyright © 2019 by Timus Radford-Mathurin.

All rights reserved.
No part of this book may be reproduced or used
in any manner without written permission of the copyright
owner except for the use of quotations in a book review.

ISBN 9781706449409

Printed in Poland
by Amazon Fulfillment
Poland Sp. z o.o., Wrocław